Committed to Fitness and a Healthy Lifestyle

How to Unleash Your Inner Motivation, Change Your Mindset and Transform Your Body Fast!

By Marta Tuchowska

Copyright © 2014, 2016

www.HolisticWellnessProject.com

www.AlkalineDietLifestyle.com

All information in this book has been carefully researched and checked for factual accuracy. However, the author and publishers make no warranty, expressed or implied, that the information contained herein is appropriate for every individual, situation or purpose, and assume no responsibility for errors or omission. The reader assumes the risk and full responsibility for all actions, and the author will not be held liable for any loss or damage, whether consequential, incidental, and special or otherwise that may result from the information presented in this publication.

Contents

INTRODUCTION

ABOUT ME AND THIS BOOK

If you are looking for a dynamic, motivational read to overcome procrastination and you wish to commit yourself to wellness, you will find this book helpful. I have created it to keep you motivated during the fitness and weight loss program that you have set for yourself. You can also use it if you are looking for a healthier lifestyle and wish to keep on track. It's a short reminder that we all need when procrastination tries to spoil our wellness efforts.

It will also help you get and stay motivated with other goals in all areas of your life. Not only one. I want to teach you what I call: "The universal success and motivation mindset". Once you've mastered it, it will always be yours.

Aside from the actual methods, my book also aims to offer you some practical tips on how to successfully apply the methods in your daily life. My personal experiences are included throughout the book; I hope you won't find them too boring!

You will learn how to make your wellness and fitness routine an inseparable part of your lifestyle and how to stay committed to it forever. You will forget about procrastination, lack of motivation, and putting your workouts and diets off "until tomorrow" and you will be able to take massive action to be truly successful at achieving your wellness goals. Celebrities, public figures, health professionals, and wellness coaches all have some strategies that result in unlocking unlimited motivation. First of all, none of them is perfect and they admit it themselves. Remember, perfection does not exist. You need to learn to focus on progress instead.

This is why I am now addicted to fitness and body work in general, even though I used to hate it. You see, I changed my beliefs about it. I used to perceive my workouts as a boring and daunting task. <u>Now, fitness is a part of who I am</u>. Instead of seeing it as something that I don't want to do but have to, I see it as something that I don't have to do but WANT to. I get immense levels of satisfaction from it. The fitter I become, the more I want to progress in my fitness efforts. However, it's not only about my body. I truly enjoy the holistic change that occurs in me as I get committed to <u>the process</u> of transforming myself. As a result, I get more satisfaction from what I do that results in what I call "automatic motivation." I don't have to think about doing physical activity or eating healthy, I just do it. Here's how you can trick your brain to do it too:

1. During this process, you will develop your emotional muscles and you will feel more connected with your mind. Fitness will also be your meditation and your moments of connectedness with the here and now.

2. As you keep yourself committed to this process, you will become a source of inspiration to others. Your passion for health and fitness will be infectious. In other words, you will be an example to other people. They will get this fitness "virus" and spread it even further. Healthy and balanced people are happy people. This is what the twenty-first century world needs. So this can be your mission. I know that some of you may find it stupid, but it's just my way of unleashing unlimited motivation levels. <u>If you try to motivate others through your own actions, you will also be more motivated yourself</u> to take more action, right?

3. You will have a strong sense of responsibility. This works closely with what I have mentioned in point two and this is how I have managed to reprogram myself. You will realize that if you don't carry on your healthy lifestyle, someone may not get exposed to it and as a result may not get inspired to take action that could help them change their quality of life.

In other words, the way I see it is this: If I don't go to the gym, someone may be out there sad and overweight. Someone might be out there going to bed depressed and overwhelmed by their negative emotions that stop them from taking action and transforming their body.

That is also one of the reasons why I am writing this book now. I feel like it is my responsibility. It may be your responsibility too if you want to. It's up to you if you feel like catching the ball I am just about to throw to you.

Also, before we start I want to make sure that you realize one thing: I am not a guru. I am a "do-ru." My mission is to inspire you through my own lifestyle so that you can create your own way. I also like sharing my situations of failure and my own mistakes. I am just a human being.

I believe in self-coaching and I want you to learn how to become your own coach so that you don't depend on any external factors to keep motivated and on track.

Also, I am not telling you what to do. I am telling you what I do. Take what you feel may work for you and reject the rest. If there is something you disagree with, please let me know. I always respect other people's beliefs and opinions and I also hope that they will respect mine in return.

Constant work is the key to progress. There are many strategies that can help you make this "regular work" a really enjoyable experience. My objective is to make them as simple to you as possible so that you can easily motivate yourself to achieve what you have always thought was impossible … well, not anymore. Motivation is a key to success, no matter what you do. And nothing is impossible.

Now let's get started on our motivation training. Thanks for taking interest in this book. I hope you enjoy it!

Disclaimer: After reading this book, you may find yourself working out without even realizing it. The gym bag will just take you to your fitness class. Another side effect that this read can cause is that you will do exactly the opposite of what your brain tells you (usually our brain tells us not to go the gym and to have a juicy kebab instead!). Another possible side effect is that you will become a source of inspiration for other people and will be able to help them too. If you know that the above-mentioned side effects can dramatically transform your life and you prefer to stay where you are, I suggest you abstain from reading this book now. I forgot to tell you that your juicer will be working overtime and your fridge will be full of healthy foods ...

Are you ready for some long-term wellness commitment? No "one-night stands" here, wellness is looking for a serious relationship with you! Yes! The time is now or never.

My Personal Story

Let me introduce myself: My name is Marta. I am thirty-one years old, and until four years ago I struggled with losing weight, gaining weight, and keeping myself healthy in general. My main problem was that I was trying to be healthy but I would always encounter some diets that did not work and would just spoil the whole process. I also suffered from low energy levels and had no zest for life. I found that the key to losing weight and keeping it off through a healthy lifestyle lies in one thing: motivation. More specifically, motivation that is distributed throughout the journey to achieving health through exercise and nutrition.

One more thing: I was never severely overweight or anything, it's just that I had a few extra kilos that would never go away no matter how hard I tried. And I also felt like a weakling. I just wanted to be healthy, feel good in my body, and burn some fat.

I always thought that being disgusted with myself was enough to keep me motivated and reach my fitness and weight loss goals. I truly believed that if I was unhappy enough, the change would come.

What I learned is that it's not about fad diets, gym memberships complete with personal training, workout campaigns that promised results or counting calories. Nothing of that stuff will work long-term. You must do it yourself. You need to change your lifestyle.

Sometimes it's not even that much about choosing the right avenue ... the truth is that even the right avenue can let you down. Even the healthiest of diets and exercise routines can fail. I know people who spend thousands of dollars on nutritionists and personal trainers. Still, they are not able to achieve their wellness and fitness goals. I figured that all the methods I had tried were not for me if I didn't learn how to keep committed to change and to stop negative, limiting thinking.

Again, the best advice I can give you is: you can become your own coach.

I would gain more weight back (or at least how much I had lost) after each failed venture. I assumed that I had just not found the right fit. Either I had picked a scam, hired someone inexperienced, or just not found that magical thing that was going to make me successful in losing weight, becoming physically fit, and achieving overall wellness.

Little did I realize that the change needed to be in *me*, <u>in my brain</u>. I had to change the way I approached my goals. I was my own downfall, while at the same time I was the person who could make me successful.

I struggled with depression and had no zest for life in my early twenties: excuse number one for not losing weight. I, as a child, used to be very active and even into my teens was an athlete, involved in kickboxing. I thought that the reason I might have been putting on weight or was not as physically fit (*fit* means able to keep up my workouts) was due to my age: excuse number two.

I was unknowingly my own worst enemy. I had no clue how success was achieved. I then happened upon a Tony Robbins motivational book, and it sparked my interest. I had to know how I could become successful through practical steps. I looked up many videos and books on success. This is when I realized that the only person to point my finger at was me. I could not blame anyone. The things that were destroying my chances of success were not diets that do not work or pills that were not formulated properly. The things that I had been missing were motivation and the tools to stay motivated.

I especially enjoyed one thing that I read in one of Tony Robbins' books. He said that there was a guy who quit smoking after several sessions (or a program) with him (Tony Robins). However, when they met several months later, it turned out that the guy got back to smoking again and blamed Tony for his failure. This is when Tony realized something that he also shares in his book ...

You must do it yourself. Let me quote his words. Real game changer!

"You and I have to become our own counsellors and master our own lives. **The second belief that you and I must have if we're going to create long-term change is that we're responsible for our own change, not anyone else**. In fact, there are three specific beliefs about responsibility that a person must have if they're going to create long-term change:

1) First, we must believe, "Something must change (...)
2) Second, we must not only believe that things must change, but we must believe, "I must change it."(...)
3) Third, we have to believe, "I can change it." (...)
Without these three core beliefs, I can assure you that any change you make stands a good chance of
being only temporary."- Tony Robbins, "Re-Awaken the Giant Within"

Suddenly, I was feeling motivated. I understood the gist of the motivation that still keeps me going. I was encouraged and compelled to find out how to keep this feeling going. I researched many different successful people who had achieved their own goals (weight loss and others). I mimicked what they had done and made it applicable to my own life. I planned ahead; this time, I was sure that I would not fail. The diet that I really took to was the alkaline diet. What I especially enjoyed was the fact that it wasn't just a diet, it was a holistic lifestyle where all the systems must go. It resonated with me as it coincided with some personal and professional changes that I was undergoing. I was so grateful I discovered this information. I began to apply it step by step and it gave me more energy to commence my fitness journey.

This happened two years ago. I lost unwanted fat and put on muscle. I have a very low body fat percentage now, and I have the stamina of an athlete. I cannot say that I have not slipped up—I have. But I have NEVER failed since I began working on my motivation.

Now, I very often go running up hills. It gives me the sensation of fulfillment. Sometimes I do it twice a day. Ever since I did it, I have never had anxiety. It gets erased during my regular "up the hill" run. I usually encounter some people who do the same, who jog on the local hills. We exchange our experiences; I very often ask them why they do it. They usually have the same reason that I do. They work on their mind while doing this.

It's only by doing things that nobody else wants to do that you will be accumulating personal success. Big changes will start from there. So while everyone is chilling in a bar during happy hour or watching reality shows and getting stuffed with unhealthy foods, you are different, my friend. You make a conscious decision to be in the one percent of the population who actually want to create their own lifestyles. My tip: Don't think about it. Just do it. Reprogram yourself. Doing what other people don't want to so means success. Instant success. Getting started means success. Plus, it's fun.

Your mind is stronger than you believe. I know mine was. I never truly understood the power of positive thinking and really believing in myself, until I studied what actually goes into being motivated.

I honestly believed, ignorantly, that either you were motivated, or you were not. I thought that some people had it, while others just did not. I had no clue that we all have the ability inside ourselves to succeed at everything. I just needed the proper tools and steps for success in order to foster and nurture that ability within myself. I found out that every human being has the innate capability to succeed in whatever thing they choose. I only needed to change my mindset. Then I was able to keep *myself* motivated.

The strategies included in this book are actual practical tools that really work. I used the same ones to get me motivated before I started my new routine. I consistently applied the tools to my daily, weekly, and monthly routines to keep my motivation levels high. I combined practical steps and things I thought might be of little significance but ended up making all of the difference in the world! By combining the practical with the psychological, I was able to win this time! I succeeded in achieving actual wellness. I have never been happier or more content. You can experience the same sense of achievement and physical wellness and health! What are we waiting for? Let's get started!

YOUR 3 FREE GIFTS

Before we get into motivation, I would like to offer you 3 free complimentary PDF eBooks and free access to my wellness and health newsletter. It will help you achieve your health goals faster (and keep on track!)

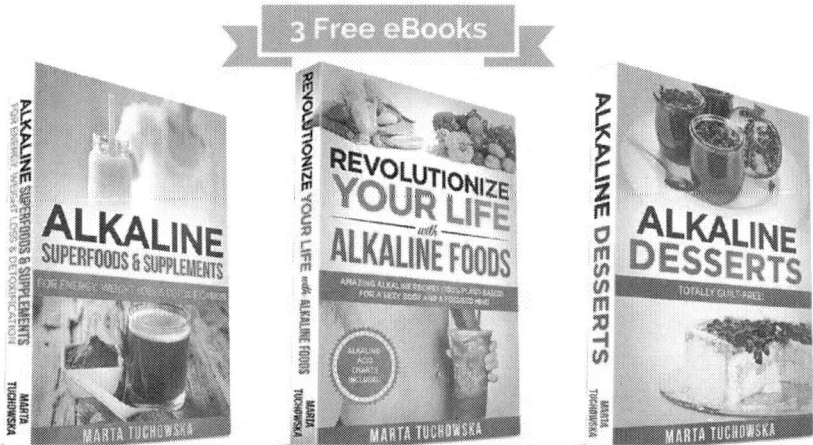

You can join at no cost and get your 3 free eBooks at:
www.HolisticWellnessProject.com/alkaline

You will also be notified about my new books at a discounted price, as well as freebies, giveaways and more health and wellness information to help you look and feel amazing!

Chapter 1 Be Successful Before You Start!

Very often, a major factor in being successful at anything is planning and preparation. Preparation itself can lead to motivation, I have found. In planning and preparing, my focus was on how to achieve my goals. Focusing on your goal and planning the tools that you are going to use to get there and achieve it is very motivating. The more prepared you feel, the more confident you will be. If I go into something knowing that I have all of the tools to make it happen, I will succeed. Like Ben Franklin once said, "By failing to prepare, you are preparing to fail."

The act of reading this chapter alone is a motivational tool. It will help you to boost your confidence, because you will find methods that will enable you to reach your goal. Don't neglect this step. It will be a time saver in the long run, even though now, you should quite naturally devote some time to prepare yourself properly for your journey.

Otherwise it's like going camping with no compass, sleeping bag, or tent, not to mention the mosquito repellent. Imagine that you do it, just hoping that you will be successful in finding a shelter. My tip is: Be prepared and make sure you have your own shelter.

Motivation for Preparation Phase

Preparation for any actual fitness or weight loss activity may seem such a daunting task for you. However, with the right type of attitude in preparation, you will simply breeze through the entire thing. This section will discuss some of the ways that you can motivate yourself during the preparation phase.

Wellness before Weight Loss

First, you need to place wellness before your desire to lose weight, gain muscle, or transform your body. (I know lots of guys who are obsessed with putting on muscle and very often experiment with plenty of random diets and supplements that are just not healthy and put lots of stress on their bodies.)

If you get obsessed about losing weight (*only* about losing weight), you will be damaging your mental and emotional health and making the whole process much more complicated. In turn, this can significantly increase the risk of having a rebound weight gain. As soon as you lose weight you are back to the same old routine and the vicious circle begins. Trust me, I have been there many times myself. Do I want to go back there? Of course I don't. I have chosen health and healthy weight as well as long-term success. I choose the same for you, my dear reader. This is why your objective number one should be: I want to be as healthy as possible! After that, you can move to achieving your weight loss goals.

Health is all we have. Otherwise there is no energy and no motivation. Health should never be the price for success, whether it's for your body transformation or social or financial goals. You need to set your health first; the most successful people in the world do. Take Tony Robbins (or other motivational speakers) for example. He never stops. He travels the world, inspiring people. One of the things he teaches is that a person should take care of their health.

Turning your focus to wellness changes your mindset—well it did for me. I no longer looked at my new alkaline nutritional program as a "diet." Instead, I looked at it as a <u>lifestyle change</u> to achieve health. By changing one word, I was able to even further motivate myself before I had even begun. Not only would I be able to wear the clothes I wanted to and look good in them, I would be *healthy*.

I was not changing my goal; I was changing the <u>way I looked at my goal</u>. I even created a mini ritual where I would talk to myself (aloud or in my head, both are fine) and visualize how my healthy lifestyle can change my life on other levels, even how it can influence my focus, my creativity, my relationships, my social life, and my finances. I associated lots of pleasure to my new alkaline diet (in your case it may be something different, choose whatever works for you) and regularly repeated my mini rituals and connected with my subconscious (just talking to myself), being able work with all my senses and all my emotions. My rituals became something like my personal motivation. I would even imagine some friends asking me about what I do, that I brim with energy constantly. I would explain to them my new lifestyle—not "just a diet".

Now, my dream is reality. People ask me what I eat and how I got started on my balanced and transformational lifestyle.

By dedicating ten to fifteen minutes a day to planning things in my mind, I was able to take control again and create my reality and my healthy way of living. The more I would do it, the more ecstatic and motivated I would feel. What really worked well for me was that I would also imagine talking to other people and motivating them. Well, this is what I am doing now, pretty much every day! I really urge you to try it yourself. Even if now you feel skeptical thinking that I am proposing some hippie-dippie stuff, please promise me that you won't reject it before you try.

In order to succeed at achieving one's goals (not only health, but also other areas of your life), a person needs information, inspiration, and motivation that will create an internal drive that I like to call a "kick in the ass." Sometimes the kick in the ass may be external. For example, you realize how unhealthy you eat after someone tells you, or you are working out at the gym and you see that seventy-year-olds are doing better than you do even though you are only thirty. External motivation is an extra push which is awesome. However, it is your work to cultivate your internal motivation. Once you have mastered it, you will be able to light your internal fire and be successful at everything. Yes, at everything! You will also stop blaming circumstances (the gym is too far way, it's raining today, I like cheese because it makes me feel good, my parents did not teach me to eat healthy, and so on). The sordid truth is, the only person in the world you can blame is you.

By the way, most people think that talking to yourself is a sign of going mad. I think the opposite. If you are in a relationship with someone, you need to learn how to communicate with him or her—in other words, you need to talk. If you want to be successful, you need to establish a thriving relationship with yourself. This is a priority. Don't be afraid to have dialogues with yourself. Be honest with yourself; honesty and honest feedback lead to improvement and progress, and this is what we want. At the same time, don't overdo it. Some people get trapped in analyzing what they did well or wrong, but in the end don't take any further action to actually implement what they have learned.

Paradigm Shift

Another way to help you stay motivated during the preparation is to give up the mentality that you have to be a perfect person when it comes to motivation for fitness and weight loss. During different phases in your fitness and weight loss activities, you will have those moments of weakness. When these happen, you should learn how to forgive yourself. After that, you should learn something out of the experience so you will know how to deal with the situation in case it happens again. Beating yourself up will only make things worse. You should use the experience of failing at something to learn as much as you can. I always say that it's not the end of the world: The good thing about getting off track is that you can always get back on it feeling even stronger. I believe that each failure makes us stronger. In other words, if you know how to use failure, you will grow.

Just like when someone criticizes you, you can ask them to hit you stronger, as you can take it!

Every time I set out to lose a bit of weight or do my fitness just for my overall health and stamina, I ended up failing. Instead of picking myself up, brushing myself off, and jumping back on the wagon, I would simply give up. One minor setback does not

29

mean you have failed. I learned that every day and every hour is another opportunity for me to keep plugging away at my weight loss and fitness goal. I had to be my own biggest cheerleader, instead of my own worst enemy. Once I learned how to do this, I was well on my way to achieving weight loss, becoming physically fit. And you can too!

Rome wasn't built in a day.

I always add that it needed much, much more than one day. But remember ... there is no reason to wait years until your "Rome of wellness success" magically builds itself. Things just don't do themselves. If you want to create your own Rome, you should commit yourself to becoming your own architect.

The truth is that no one else will do it for you. Even if you can afford the most expensive coach, the moment the goal is achieved and the coach is gone, chances are you will be slowly getting back to where you were before.

Don't perceive health and fitness as a chore. Don't look at your goals as something that is supposed to add to your willpower only. I am not saying that cultivating your willpower is bad, but there is a risk of looking at your goals as something that needs to be completed even though you hate it.

You need to give yourself a gift to fall in love with your new routine. Repeat it constantly. This is a very important step. It's also about giving your workouts bigger meaning. Make it juicy. Know your WHY behind your actions.

For example, instead of just saying "my goal is to work out at the gym every day for one hour," your subconscious will perceive it as something more attractive if you say "I am committed to going to the gym and working not only on my body but also on my mind. My actions of commitment inspire other people. This is my mission. I can't give up! I am grateful for who I become in the process, as I also develop my emotional muscles. As my body gets fitter and fitter, my mind gets stronger and stronger."

You can also add a reward that will be waiting for you to celebrate your new choices of being committed to wellness. For example, once a month you can go shopping for new clothes. Imagine the feeling of joy of actually trying out new clothes and looking at a healthier, fitter, sexier, more energized (please add as many adjectives as you can think of, I am just providing you with what I do and the verbal power that works for me) you in the mirror at your favorite store.

Grab that feeling. Try to keep it and make a decision to feel that way now. Imagine how you would walk, talk, and act if this was happening already. It depends only on you.

Goal Setting

Goal setting is another important aspect of the preparation phase. In writing down what you plan to achieve in the long run, you should make sure that these are reasonable. Moreover, these goals should be objective so you will know if you are close enough to achieving them. In this regard, you should formulate simpler goals from your long-term list to make them more attainable. Accomplishing the short-term goals can significantly improve your motivation even more.

I set one main goal for every day, one for every week, and one for every month. That way I could actually feel accomplished on a regular basis. As I reached the smaller goals, my self-esteem and motivation snowballed. I was able to achieve momentum and felt like I was actually getting somewhere. The more progress I saw (I realized I had muscles that I knew existed only from anatomy books I studied when doing training in massage therapy!), the more it would light my internal motivational fire. I have come to conclusion that less can be better sometimes. Perseverance is the key. Some people (including myself a few years ago) go to the gym and just kill themselves, and they can't move the following day or two. Now, I am all up for pushing your limits. But I wouldn't suggest you let those limits push you so that you start experiencing exaggerated amounts of pain and even injury that will only put you off track. Don't take on more than you can take. If you have never exercised before, I suggest you join the gym and ask one of the trainers to design a program for you. My local gym offers it for free (they also ask you to do regular checkups with a doc) and I took advantage of it. The problem is that many people are too ashamed to ask. I always say that everyone has to start at some point. Those guys and gals who work there are there because they want to help you. They won't laugh at you because you have low stamina or are overweight. If they can help someone make the first move, they go home after work filling fulfilled.

This is why you should never be afraid to ask questions at the gym.

YouTube, blogs, DVDs, and other programs are complementary and work more for those who already know their bodies, strengths, and weaknesses and use those recorded workouts as source of motivation or inspiration.

If only someone had told me this a few years ago! I wasted so much time and energy thinking I was moving towards my goals, but I was actually working out beyond my endurance, in a way that it was too much for my body to take.

I had to learn to be patient and consistent.

Another mistake that I would constantly repeat when I was younger was to resort to energy drinks and stimulants with caffeine so as to work out more. I would not recommend this path.

I can now say that I am a fitness girl, but I am also a yoga girl. What I learned from my yoga practice is that you have to learn to listen to your body.

You also need to go deeper than that. Listen to your emotions. Work on your mindset.

I like to work out to sweat out negative feelings, emotions, and anger (these are human feelings). It's a much healthier option that indulging in alcohol and other toxic substances. However (a very big however), by learning to dig deep, I refer to the ability to connect to your mind and emotions. Fitness is healthy in general, but I also know many fitness people who are not really that healthy, even though they look fit, sexy, and shredded. They are putting too much strain on their bodies and as a result, they may become obsessed with their looks—just like people who get addicted to sun beds. At some point, the body will rebel.

What is fitness to me now?

To put it simply: It's about overcoming yourself and pursuing wellness. Fitness is a tool that if properly used can help you achieve wellness. However, if abused, it can take your wellness away.

This is why if you don't want to end up in frustration or in emotional pain, getting caught in the vicious circle, you will need your own workout plans.

Let's dive into it.

Workout Plans

Preparing your workout plans at least one month from the actual implementation day can help boost your motivation. For one thing, this can make you look forward to something. Also, this can help add more structure and a depth in priority for your plans. You may write them down on a sheet of paper or save the plans in your smartphone or tablet. Make sure that you go through your workout plans on a regular basis; personally I have a look at mine every day or at least every other day! Like I suggested before, you may ask a fitness professional to lend you a hand. You will save your precious time and allocate your energy in the right direction straight away.

For myself, I would always have a backup workout. One of my previous trainers had suggested this years ago. I had never put it into practice, but guess what? It really works. I used to think that working out at home is something stupid. What a limiting belief! Working out at home is a skill that you can develop and you can do it anytime you want and everywhere you want, even when you travel. A couple of years ago I joined Pilates classes and learned the basics. It would also add more variety to my workouts and save my time (I did not have to travel to the gym; I could just squeeze in short fifteen-minute workouts at home—no excuses!).

I think that I was subconsciously trying not to work out at home, because I knew that it is something that is harder to find exercises not to get committed to. You may skip a day at the gym because it's raining or you don't have enough time. But guess what, everyone has fifteen minutes to complete a simple workout from the comfort of their own home.

I finally accepted it and made my home workout routines my best friend.

Sure, you may have planned out your workouts every day. What happens when you do feel that lack of motivation to do it? In order to keep moving toward your goal, you should always have a <u>backup workout</u>. I chose to have a few options for the days I just did not feel like adhering to my plan. I used videos, both online and DVDs. It really helped me to have someone just tell me what to do. I did not have to coach myself when I was feeling "bleh" or have to get up and out of the house to go to the gym or for a run. Also, I had two different lengths of videos, those over forty minutes and those that were twenty to twenty-five minutes. This ensured that even if I was tired, I still could get in a workout. Sure, it was not a super workout, but a workout nonetheless. It helped me to know that I did *something.* By giving myself a <u>safety net</u>, I was able to feel accomplished even if I did not adhere to my original plan. I also learned that by preparing a few different options to choose from, I would feel more spontaneous and could actually pick up something that would suit a given moment. Sometimes it works better than just following through the same old plan. There also might be some unexpected circumstances, for example when your friend asks you to help her move houses, or it's raining, or you suddenly have to go to the bank to sort something out. It's good to have a plan B, C, D, and even E. I also have my "short but sweet and effective plan" which is a short Pilates-inspired workout at home (I may also follow a DVD).

Focus

As much as you want to boost your motivation immediately, you should make sure that you will not force yourself to focus on all your goals at the same time. If you are not used to the change, you may start off changing at least one or two habits first. Once you get the hang of those, you may incorporate more changes in your lifestyle. Doing this little by little can help you appreciate your success even more. Thus, you can get more motivated. It is way more important to focus on the process rather than on the results.

Focus only on one thing. Just one thing. You practice mindfulness by doing it.

Apart from that, it is essential that you enjoy the process, e.g., "I feel great and really refreshed after my thirty-minute jog this morning!" instead of saying, "O no! I have lasted only for half an hour, whereas my goal is to be able to jog for at least one hour! I am not fit at all!"

If you choose the second option, you won't get as successful in the long run as you want to be and you may experience losing your motivation. Moreover, you will be too strict on yourself and eventually quit your workouts, saying, "I wasn't born with stamina ..." (I forbid you to go for this excuse!)

This is why you should always try to focus on the process and your little achievements. You should also be happy about them and always say to yourself, "Another successful workout!" or "Another successful healthy morning!"

Once you have managed to control your focus, the ultimate wellness success will be yours!

Alternatives

It is also advisable to have alternative plans ready. During your fitness and weight loss endeavors, you will most likely encounter some setbacks along the way. According to experts, preparing some alternative plans can help boost your motivation to commit to your original plan all over again.

For example, if you have a weak day, instead of indulging in your excuses and missing out another day at the gym, at least try to go for a walk. If you have some problems sticking to your diet, allow yourself a little cheat but finish off by eating healthy. Let's say that in the afternoon you treated yourself to a piece of cake. Don't worry too much about it, think of it as a treat and as for dinner, try to prepare some healthy and juicy salad or make a green alkaline smoothie. Just because you cheated once that day does not mean that the entire day is ruined! Have those alternatives planned in case something happens, but don't abuse them and don't use them as your main plan. I am not defending laziness; I just aim for a healthy balance and mental health. I have a friend who ended up with a severe case of bulimia as a result of being too strict with herself. This is why I really underline the importance of mental health when it comes to weight loss or fitness efforts. You have had that cake, so what? Relax, no one is going to die. It has already happened; now, it's all about NOW! Just figure out how to fix it. Maybe you should work out more? There is a solution to everything so don't cry over spilled milk. As Tony Robbins says, "The past does not equal to future. It's what you decide to do right NOW that matters."

Goal Improvements

If your plans are proceeding as you have originally intended, you should make sure that you will work on improving your goals. This includes adjusting them according to the changes that occur during your weight loss and fitness activities.

Recognizing your potential to go far into the fitness and weight loss program can help instantly boost your morale. If you are preparing for a whole new cycle for the entire program, it will also be helpful if you can point out some emerging positive qualities that you have managed to develop during the previous phases. From these things, you may challenge yourself farther by setting up increasingly more difficult goals.

Goal improvement also includes adding new goals as you accomplish the smaller, short-term goals. As I progressed, I would make my weekly goal a little bit more challenging. This enabled me to do two things:

1. I gained more self-confidence which meant more motivation—I knew that I was capable since I had accomplished so much already day to day.

2. It encouraged me to reach deeper within myself to make each goal a tiny bit more challenging.

For example, when doing my uphill run and successfully accomplishing it, my mind would challenge me about doing it again. This is extra work that will help you feel more self-confident and actually see that practice makes perfect! Of course, like I said earlier, first make sure that this extra effort won't be too much for your body to take—we don't want any injuries. Still, if running up the hill again is too much, your additional challenge can be to walk around for thirty minutes. You still move your body and eliminate toxins. Plus, if you do it in nature—which I really recommend—you also heal and energize yourself.

Nature is free, and it also forms part of being committed to wellness.

Negative Conditioning

To help you mentally prepare and motivate yourself, you should also resort to negative conditioning. This simply means that you have to list the negative effects that you can suffer from if you do not work on achieving your health-related goals. Writing down the consequences of not sticking to your plans can help you work more on your plans. Examples of that are: "I won't fit in my clothes or I will be tired all the time," "I won't be a role model for other people," and "I won't be able to show off a slim, sexy body the way I have always wanted."

Make it personal. Use your imagination and employ all the emotions and feelings. Pain is really powerful, and our human nature will do everything to avoid it.

Formulating Visions

Creating a vision can also help you picture yourself and project your goals to the final result. You may further make the vision more meaningful by describing how these things can make you appear, feel, and move once you have achieved them.

For instance, this vision:

I will feel great just wearing what I want and having unlimited levels of energy. I will feel so proud of myself and all the hard work that went into transforming my body. My family and friends will be very happy for me and they will congratulate me on my success. I will be perceived as a healthy and fit person and a wellness expert!

It will help you feel committed. Trust me!

It is my hope that this chapter helped you see that a little planning and preparation go a long way in getting motivated. You should be very excited; excitement alone is enough to get one motivated. So there you go, you are already on your path to success!

Chapter 2 Unlimited Motivation for Wellness

Getting motivation up before you start your program is important, but keeping up your process of change is even more important. You must keep up your willpower, determination, and perseverance in order to succeed. You must constantly remind yourself what your vision and main goal are and how your daily sections bring you closer or farther away from your ultimate goal. You must constantly improve your motivation as you are making progress. This will partially happen naturally. As you go, you will start to see results that are motivating. You will get into a routine, and that will also help your motivation levels.

Make sure though that you add to your storage of willpower, motivation, and excitement about what you do along the way. Enjoy the process and who you're becoming as a result. Many people are too fixated on the result only and forget about the pleasure of the journey. It's good to know where you're going and where your final destination is. However, you must also learn the process of "traveling" and how to enjoy it. When you master it, you can choose new destinations (that is, new health and fitness goals as well as other goals) and get there without any problems. If you do not keep replenishing it you will run low. That will only discourage you. Keeping your motivation high will help you to increase your willpower at the same time.

Motivation for the Actual Program

After this chapter, you will understand some of the motivational techniques that you can implement during the actual fitness and weight loss program. Keeping these things in mind will help you improve your focus on your ultimate goal. This can also increase your success rate in getting the figure that you have always wanted.

A few years ago, little did I know about utilizing the power of the subconscious mind. I had a friend who told me about vision boards, but I would reject it as something stupid and new age. Now I understand that I was deeply mistaken. Not long ago I called that friend of mine and I actually thanked him for inspiration and apologized for calling him a freak.

It is my intention to make it infectious. It's why I am writing this book. I am throwing you a ball, remember?

If you create a vision board for yourself (or, like I do now, even a few of them) your subconscious mind will be exposed to them on a regular basis—even if your conscious mind is switched off. Don't reject it before you try it.

I am now in the process of creating more vision boards for myself to manifest other goals as well as a lifestyle I want to create for myself. It keeps me motivated first thing in the morning. It serves me as a reminder and as a big WHY.

Knowing Yourself

Another way that can get you across the actual process of workouts and diet regimens is to know yourself as an individual. In line with this, you should also know why you are making the fitness-related changes that you are implementing at the moment. Instead of working against your natural tendencies, you should use your positive traits to your advantage as much as possible.

You can pick workouts that you like. Pick a sport you would actually like to try or already know you excel at. I love hiking and it truly is an awesome workout. I got a new membership to the closest regional park and would make it a point to hike once or twice a week. Being able to do something you like or something that you are good at will only boost your motivation level that much more.

Choose foods that you love, only pick healthier versions. For myself, I love Asian food, especially Chinese. So instead of doing without, I created a few meals that I knew would be tasty for me and healthy at the same time. That way, when I was craving Chinese, I could make my healthy recipe instead of going for takeout. It was just one more way that I kept myself motivated. I knew my weaknesses and prepared backup plans so that I would not fail!

I have committed myself to turning my weaknesses into my assets and learning from them.

Proper Pacing

Doing too many activities at the same time can spell disaster for you in the long run. Instead of doing tasks that do not really appeal much to you, you should perform actions one small step at a time. Accomplishing these small things can do much for your motivation levels. Additionally, these are more realistic than aiming for bigger things in one fell swoop.

My Mistake

Do not put the cart before the horse, as this can be disastrous for self-esteem, which is intrinsically linked to motivation. For example, when I began my motivationally fueled workout and nutritional workout plan, I made a huge mistake. I signed up for a 10k marathon. I figured it would be challenging and help me to reach my goals. Big mistake. I did not give myself enough time to reach a fitness level where I could actually have pulled it off successfully. I ended up falling to the ground about halfway through, red-faced and gasping for air. Both literally and figuratively, I had not paced myself. I had not planned ahead enough to give myself enough time to be able to physically accomplish this goal. Yet I did not make the same self-sabotaging move that I had made in the past when this happened. I did not give up. I used it as a learning experience and planned ahead the next time. Still, I don't want you to repeat my mistakes.

But even if you do make a mistake, use it to your advantage and learn from it. Learn as much as you can.

Over the next six months I planned out my training, both week to week and month to month. My previous failure at pacing myself motivated me to succeed. I was determined that I would reach my goal of finishing a 10k. Guess what? With proper planning this time, by pacing myself along the way and using my failure to muster up a surplus of willpower, I was able to finish the 10k. I was successful! Planning and pacing yourself will enable you to be ultimately more motivated.

Moderation

For your food items, you should moderate your intake but never eliminate them altogether. Getting rid of your favorite food will only make you crave more for them. You may resort to small portions of these food items and create healthier alternatives to address your craving issues. If you have no idea about the food items that you can use for substitution, you should check out some online resources or reading materials so you can get some good ideas.

I do have my favorite cheat food, which are Spanish tapas. Now, I do the alkaline diet, and tapas are acidic. However, since I eat healthy, I am balanced and energetic. I know that every now and then, I can have this little cheat meal when I go out with my Spanish friends , I have some *patatas bravas* and fried *calamares* and other food that I usually stay away from, but I do it really occasionally. Plus, I enjoy the time out I spend with my friends. I also know how to get back on the healthy track. I never cook or eat these foods at home. This little cheating ritual also makes me realize that I am not depriving myself of anything. Eating those foods is not my lifestyle, only an occasional treat.

This is something that I recommend only when you are already settled with your diet and feeling confident about it. If you have been indulging in unhealthy, toxic foods or fast foods for years, you need to commit yourself to a clean, detoxifying diet first. High energy levels to work out, focus, clean skin, and weight loss are all the benefits you can reap off.

As far as moderation goes, when exercising on a regular basis make sure not to overdo it. Do not try to push yourself every day for hours on end, especially at the beginning. For myself, I could not endure a full forty-minute workout when I began. My friend, who was also a trainer, suggested that I work out twenty minutes in the morning and another twenty in the evening. Exercise must be done at your own physical level. If you try to do something that you are incapable of, you will lose motivation. If you try to exercise in excess, it can easily result in injury. That would be a sure-fire way to *lose* motivation.

I do have a few friends who are incredibly fit and I envy them of their endurance. They very often work out for three to four hours a day. But this has been their lifestyle for a really long time and they know what they're doing. I set them as my example. Even if you have already succeeded with your original goals, you need to carry on and set another goal, making it more and more difficult. Surrounding yourself with people you look up to is a strategy that I use constantly. They are my role models, my gurus, my coaches, and my mentors! They have achieved what I am willing to achieve.

This is what true coaching is all about.

Avoid "coaches" who have no personal achievements, no matter how many certifications they have accumulated.

Simplicity

Actually, avoiding quick fixes for your food and drink items can help you significantly lower your calorie intake. As soon as you see the results of cutting down on these fixes, you will surely get more motivated. For instance, instead of drinking soda to quench your thirst, you may simply opt for water as a healthy alternative. Instead of grabbing the chips, have fresh cut veggies or fruits at your disposal. Hungry while in the car? Instead of hitting the nearest unhealthy fast food drive-through, pull out the bag of trail mix that you planned ahead and prepared for the car! I know that this is pretty basic. But I must admit that even though I knew it pretty well, I did not take it into action.

"To know and not to apply it really not to know"--Jim Rohn

*H*ealthy Snacks

Get into the habit of choosing healthy snacks. Start carrying around healthy snacks such as fruits, nuts, carrots, almond drinks, green tea, etc. to make sure that you can distract yourself from hunger. If you are working out intensively, go for snacks like bananas, dried-fruit bars, or natural yoghurt to make sure that your energy levels stay high and that you are always in the mood for more exercise. If you are at home, try to invest some time in preparing fresh juices and smoothies at least once a day. You will be amazed by the results! I have even gotten into the habit of snacking on raw carrots and cucumbers. Cucumbers are highly alkaline and refreshing. They hydrate your body and provide you with minerals.

Some people at the gym would look really strangely at me snacking on raw cucumbers between one workout and another. Some people are really set in their ways. At first, I would feel ashamed to manifest my habits, but then I actually took pride in what I do, and I stuck to my own way.

Over the years, I learned that success is about doing what very few people are willing to do (or no one is willing to do).

I personally love juicing. It helps me to get a ridiculous amount of fresh, raw vegetables into my diet. Yet there are always times that I need to satiate my desire to snack. The way I make sure that I have fresh healthy options within my reach at all times is simple. Every time I go grocery shopping, I spend twenty minutes preparing my snacks. I wash and chop veggies and fruits, putting them into snack-sized baggies or containers. That way, they are right there to grab. I also take time to make a container of nut or trail mix and put it into the same-sized baggies. It only takes twenty minutes to avert a motivation-sapping disaster.

Support System

Finding a friend, a group, or a trainer with similar goals can serve as your accountability partners while you are working on your plans. If you feel like quitting halfway through your program, they can encourage you to do otherwise and can even help you do better on your workouts and diet program. They can even help you look for some meaningful ways to divert your energies from ill mindsets to productive actions.

If you can't find anyone around you, turn to an online community. This is what I do. Now here is the thing: Over the years, I have committed myself to personal development and started working on myself —my body, mind, and emotions. Many of my old friends would just say I was going crazy. They did not want to progress or be successful. They wanted to stay where they were. I accepted their choices; I don't like preaching to people. I am committed to inspiring people through my very own actions. However, be prepared that as you begin to progress, be successful, and emanate positive energy, some people (usually naysayers) will turn away from you. Some people just don't want you to be extraordinary, as it makes them look small ...

Sad, but true...

During the process of my personal and professional transformation (a topic for another book that I will surely write to share my story with you), I lost many of those "friends." I used to be sad in the beginning, as I did not do anything wrong to them. I never put them down; it was never my intention. I did care for them and wanted to help them. Then, I realized that it was meant to happen. It was actually a blessing. They were not my real friends.

Real friends stayed with me. I can count them using fingers of only one hand. I go for quality, not quantity. As my old "friends" discover their own path to self-development, I may be able to help them. For now, I will let them do what they have chosen, which is the same ol', same ol': complaining and very often indulging in toxic substances that only add to the problem.

Here comes my other tip: stay away from those who will bring you down. My mother used to always tell me that you are who you hang out with. This is true, to a certain extent. Not only will bad habits of other people appear enticing (especially when your motivation or willpower is low), some people will definitely try to bring you down. Misery does in fact love company. People may inadvertently try to sabotage you. Hang around positive, like-minded people to gain more motivation. Stay away from negative people with bad habits, for they will suck your motivation dry.

If health and fitness are your priority, find people who are on the same vibe. If you keep hanging out with skeptics, naysayers, and "all that unhealthy crowd", they might just laugh at your new routine.

However, you may also be able to inspire someone. Many people simply hide in their comfort zone, even though deep inside they want to change. Others create layers of criticism, skepticism, and even indulging in alcohol or drugs because they are scared to let the change happen. Now, you can inspire them. From my own experience, I would not recommend preaching, but when you commit yourself to achieving your goals and manifesting health, they will see that you are getting results and that whatever it is that you are doing, this "stuff" actually works.

This is how you may help someone. It's a wonderful feeling when someone decided to catch the ball, or at least tried to.

By using these motivational tips and tricks, you should be able to start making headway on your journey to wellness. You will gain motivation and replenish it regularly, which will give you momentum in the direction of achieving your physical fitness and nutritional goals.

Chapter 3 Control It! Psychological Aspects for Motivation

This chapter will present you with some of the psychologically centered motivational techniques that you can perform to help you improve your focus on your fitness-related goals. If you incorporate most of these methods regularly, you will find it easier to turn these things into habits. In essence, you will find it easier to motivate yourself.

It almost goes without saying that motivation is psychological. We get motivation internally from our spirit and brain. If you figure out your own psychology and how to change it to motivate yourself physically, you are definitely on the road to wellness and success in achieving physical fitness and health. Our psyche can actually enable us to do things that we may think we are physically incapable of. The mind is a very powerful tool for the body. If you use it to motivate yourself, the physical limits you thought you might have can be overcome.

Go Easy on Yourself

Just like I have already mentioned in the previous chapters, you should not take things too hard on yourself. Beating yourself up over small acts or even large acts of failure during your attempts will undoubtedly decrease your motivational levels. Conversely, being kind to yourself can help you stay on track. One way to do this is to enforce a reward system for every difficult task that you are bound to make.

Because it is a given fact that you cannot control every aspect of your fitness and weight loss program, you should not beat yourself up for every slip-up that happens. A good way to cope with the loss is to start off from the point where you left off.

I had to remind myself, every time that I screwed up, that progression is more important than perfection. As long as I was still trying, as long as *some* of my goals were being met, I was still making progress. Any successful person will tell you that this is very important to engrain into your psyche. This ensures that you will not self-sabotage. Every day, minute, and hour is a new opportunity to move closer to your wellness goal and succeed!

At some point, my urge for perfectionism made me feel anxious, nervous, and unfulfilled. If this ever happens to you, try to work with gratitude. Focus on what you have achieved, learned, or at least tried to achieve; focus on all your efforts. Write it all down and read it aloud. This normally does the trick for me. It erases not only anxiety but also frustration.

Part-by-Part Approach

It is also important to note that not all of the things that you have to do should boil down to the all-or-nothing concept. As in the previous point, you may resort to the reward system for each small effort that you do for your fitness and weight loss. You may tally them as you go along the tasks. After getting a predetermined number of tallies, you may exchange them for something that you want to have. This is acceptable as long as you do not ruin the rest of the goals permanently.

Personally, I chose to pick rewards that would benefit my new lifestyle and future goals. This cut out self-loathing after rewarding myself with "cheating." I would give myself rewards in the form of something that would further my progress, and in turn, further fuel my motivation. Here are some examples of rewards that I provided myself with: new workout clothes, new music to work out to, new exercise equipment, a day trip to a national park for hiking, or a dinner out at the newest restaurant featuring healthy food. These would also help me carry on with my goals and become stronger in the process.

Journal

You may also boost your morale by starting a journal about your positive experience. You may write down daily entries on how you feel healthier because of the exercise program and the diet regimen that you are in at the moment. Take it to another level and ... record it! It works. Listen to yourself.

At first I felt a bit stupid when doing this, but since I realized how powerful it is I can't stop.

I like long walks in nature and recording my voice as well as listening to it and grabbing positive emotions.

By the way, you may also do it when you have a bad day and have no one to turn to. It's human nature to have a bad day every now and then. Usually when I listen to myself having a bad day, I feel like breaking this vicious circle right away. Why? Because I believe in the law of attraction. I know that I simply can't afford to feel down.

Remember to read your journal as well. It is an awesome motivator. I would read back to when I first began. It was very encouraging to see my progress on paper. It was extremely motivating to read, in my own words, how far I had come and how much my thinking had changed. Seeing physical progress is one thing, but *reading* how my thought processes, motivation levels, and physical fitness level had progressed was another.

I have recently read my journal from two years ago. There was also my own feedback and my excitement about achieving my future goals. Now that I looked back on it, I felt like crying out of joy. What was really difficult and challenging to me back then is now a piece of cake. I am also utterly grateful that in the process of transforming my body (and also my mind) I managed to inspire others and spread positive energy.

I am sure that even some of the skeptics who would kind of laugh at me munching on raw cucumbers would have this thought if they tried it themselves.

Mental Mood Setup

It is helpful to set your current mental mood for each day. According to experts, allowing yourself to feel good will help increase the likelihood of exercise and good nutrition becoming permanent parts of your life. To help you set up a motivational mood, you may tweak some exercise routines or diet staples to make them more exciting.

My mental mood setup for the day entailed some meditation and a walk or a sit outside. I also did my daily affirmations. Yes, I felt silly at first telling myself how wonderful I was, how smart I am, etc. Yet it really works. It is very motivating being your own cheerleader. I was surprised that I could really convince myself of these things. It gave me a winning attitude at the beginning of every day, which is a major component of motivation. It worked for me. I am now in such a habit of doing this that I find myself doing it intermittently throughout the day!

I know I am being repetitive here, but I do it for a reason. I want you to start creating your own rituals. Don't be afraid to share them with others. Maybe you could even share them as a comment in the review section of this book?

Optimism

Optimism can help you go a long way. You should focus mostly on the positive things that you have done throughout the day. If negative things are bound to happen for a part of the day, you should not be discouraged. You should instead acknowledge the efforts you are exerting to get to your goals.

I used to be a pessimist. Yeah, I was the girl who said, "If you expect the worst, at least you won't be disappointed." This is what I was always told as a kid. Some of my family members are like a broken record with this line. Of course, I try to teach them my new, positive view of the world. Optimism will never hurt you and it can be of immense help. Pessimism on the other hand is always detrimental and results in feeling overwhelmed, with having nothing to look forward to and being unhappy. Pessimism will never enable you to reach your goals; optimism will. This was one key thing I had been missing every time I set out to achieve my personal wellness goals. My pessimism led to my failure. Optimism is a key component in motivation. How can you be motivated if you are always looking at the downside? By allowing yourself to be pessimistic, you only go right back to where you were before. Which can be a really dark and sad place.

Affirmation

To help enhance your motivation even more, you should make it a habit to affirm yourself with every positive thing that you do. You may do this by writing reminders of how well you have been sticking to the fitness and weight loss plans and posting them in different areas of the house. Your imagination is the only limit to what can be achieved.

Taste of Success

Getting a glimpse of what you achieve in the long run can help you improve your motivation. For instance, if you lost some weight for the first few weeks, you may focus on that achievement and perform more of the desirable behaviors that led to that result.

For me, every time I was able to fit in an outfit or size that was previously too small, I was able to get another glimpse of success. It was much more motivating for me to fit into that skirt that was too small a month ago than it was to see the result on the scale over two weeks. I also found motivation in success through my physical endurance and stamina. For example, when starting my workouts on day one, I could do one pull-up. By the end of the month I could do many sets per day! I was only able to use only five-pound dumbbells during lunges on day one, but by two weeks I was already up to ten pounds!

Eventually, motivation will be working for you on autopilot. Of course, remember to take care of it. It can always work harder for you!

There is always some minimal investment required from your part. But now you know what to do: all you need to focus on is ACTION.

Minimize Negative Self-Talks

If you are a pessimist, you should at least minimize the negative self-talks that you tend to give yourself. In the event that you start doing this, you should make sure that you will have an outlet for the action. In this regard, it is helpful to have someone reliable to talk to. You may also offer yourself a payoff if you ever get rid of this habit for good.

The easiest way that I found to minimize my negative self-talk was to recognize when I was doing it and immediately turn to positive affirmation. I would use affirmations verbally by saying them out loud. Every time I became aware that I was thinking negative things, I would counteract it with positive affirmation. You may feel a bit funny at first—I did—but by verbally commending yourself, it helps you become more aware of the negative self-talk. Eventually I was able to break my habit. Sure it looked funny to others, but that helped me to break the habit as well. It was brought to my attention and I quickly gained the habit of self-affirmation and praise.

Negative Reinforcement

Negative reinforcement also has a significant impact on your fitness and weight loss program. You may list down what will happen to you when you gain excessive weight. Because you do not wish to suffer from these consequences, you will most likely do what is necessary to prevent these from happening. Those, in effect, are forms of motivation for you. This was mentioned in the beginning of the book; however, you can use it constantly for all your goals no matter which stage of progress are they at.

Avoid Vanity-Centered Goals

The physical changes should be the last thing that you should focus on. Otherwise, this will only make you go after the vanity-related issues even more. When this happens, you can often make the mistake of succumbing to superficial means to reach your goals. In the long run, you are just fooling yourself. Because you do not enjoy the results on the long term, you will most likely lose motivation. Some people resort to surgeries to get rid of fat. They focus on a result, but most of these changes do not last long. They have not mastered the process. The same applies to money—some people inherit fortunes or win millions of dollars. Yet since they have never been in the process of making money themselves, working hard on it, investing it and managing it, they very often lose their fortunes. Result-only goals are what I call "vanity-centered" goals. If you spice it up with the process and the fun of becoming a new, more balanced version of yourself, you will be able to achieve your goal and develop holistically: mind, body, and spirit.

Change in Scenery

A change in scenery can help you change your general behavior towards what you are doing. This can also help you boost your willpower. If you are used to jogging using the treadmill, you may create some minor but interesting modifications by jogging around a nearby park. If you feel more confident than ever, you may even try out inclined surfaces to add physical challenge and a new dimension to your cardio workout.

I was an avid runner outdoors. I found that I could extend my runs and push myself to the limit by running somewhere. That way I would have to run back as well, doubling my run and motivating myself to get back home! It helped me not to become bored with my runs (treadmills and track running are good but can become monotonous). I would change my destinations regularly. You can do the same as I did and apply that idea to hikes and walks. Wherever your destination, you will have to make the trip back! This added to the amount of time I spent working out.

Active or Passive Rest

Every person needs to have some form of rest no matter what they are doing at the moment. In line with this, you should refrain from pushing yourself to your limits as much as possible. Active forms of rest such as trying out yoga or simply going passive by enjoying a massage can help you get yourself together for another bout of fitness and weight loss activities.

Unpredictable Routines

Making the exercise routines unpredictable can do wonders for your body. This is as far as the muscular and the cardiovascular changes are concerned. You may also resort to more food sharing to help you significantly cut down on your calorie intake. This will not only prove to be an interesting experience but also a healthy one.

Imitation

Reading through numerous fitness- and weight loss–related websites and magazines or watching similar television shows can help you keep on track. You can draw in some motivating ideas from the new concepts that you will learn from the discussions. In this regard, you should make sure that the shows and the reading materials that you will take advantage of are reliable. Like I mentioned in the previous chapters, you first need to get the hang of the basics; you need a platform to stand on. A professional fitness trainer/professional can help you make the first step.

Imitation is useful in any goal that you would like to achieve. Finding out the steps and strategies that successful people used to reach their goals is an invaluable tool. Look for people who have been successful in reaching their health and wellness goals and copy their tactics. This is the best way to be triumphant!

Chapter 4 Simply the Best: Motivational Techniques for the Feedback Phase

In this section, you will learn motivational techniques that you can utilize during the evaluation phase. The evaluation phase is a regular assessment of what you have achieved from the fitness and weight loss programs so far. Because of this, this phase is considered one of the most crucial points when you should boost your morale for the next wave of fitness and weight loss strategies.

Derive Advantages from Positive Actions

I stopped eating fast food and takeout on a regular basis. Not only did this help immensely when it came to avoiding unhealthy food and excess calories, it also helped my pocketbook. I saved at least thirty euros a week. I put that into a fund and at the end of the month used it to pay for my healthy and beneficial self-rewards. It was a win-win situation that was extremely helpful in my own personal motivation levels.

Monthly Feedback and Tracking Progress

During the end of each month, you may want to dedicate a few minutes of your time to providing yourself with feedback (or ask some else to do it for you) and if you see you have fallen off track, make necessary corrections. Make up for cheating or not sticking to your plan as you outlined in the beginning. This is important because staying fit and getting rid of those unwanted pounds is a long-term stint.

While you are at it, you should also monitor how far your efforts have taken you. You may do this by creating a checklist beforehand. During your actual evaluation process, you may tick off some items that you have already accomplished from the time you started.

Goal Assessment and Modifications

This is also the perfect time for you to evaluate if your goals are important to you at that point. Bring up your WHYS again. Change and adjust if necessary. People change and so do their goals. Listen to your intuition. It is equally important for you to take note of the actions and options that you have considered. Based on these things, you should make the necessary changes to improve on what you are currently doing.

Getting a fitness coach or a personal trainer can help speed up the process of changing and transforming your lifestyle. You will simply achieve your fitness or weight loss goals faster, as your coach will hold you accountable. Furthermore, a truly successful fitness coach or a personal trainer will also have a truly inspirational and healthy lifestyle, meaning that it will motivate you more than you can possibly imagine. I will leave this to you. I hope that you now feel empowered to become your own coach.

Granted, personal trainers and coaches cannot do it for you. Remember, it starts with you. Once you have that drive though, they can be a super tool in keeping you motivated and helping you find things within yourself to keep you going.

Chapter 5 Easy and Effective: Other Motivational Techniques

You may not be able to utilize all of the techniques mentioned in this chapter. However, some of them can really come in handy. This especially holds true during some of the emotionally low times when you need that added boost of inspiration.

New Items

You may buy yourself some of the stylish workout clothes and equipment that can make you look better. The concept of looking better so you can feel better plays a major role in this matter. This method can especially help you get through the difficult phases of the fitness and weight loss program more than you will ever realize. See yourself as a fitness veteran or even imagine you are a professional personal trainer and that you are actually helping others! New fitness clothes equals new fitness attitude. You will see yourself as a fit person and you will immediately take massive action.

Insight Sharing

To further enhance your support system for motivation, you may turn to your friends and loved ones. Sharing your concerns about fitness and weight loss can help you create the changes that you want to have based on your goals. These people can help you by being responsible enough to remind you if you fall short of your targets.

There are many weight and healthy lifestyle forums and groups that you can join as well, for free. It is so nice to talk to others who are looking for motivation or have knowledge to pass along. I am still a member of a few, and nothing motivates me more than to pass on what I know to others! That is part of my reason for writing this book.

Social Networking

Using your social networking accounts can serve as an outlet for your insights on what you are going through during the different fitness-related phases. This can serve as a helpful reinforcement if you have already started a journal. Posting your insights regarding your fitness journey can help you gain a stronger support system. However, if you will utilize this motivational method, you should make sure that you will not spend long periods browsing the site away. This activity in itself can lead to additional unhealthy pounds.

There are also many apps available for use with smartphones and other devices. They range from exercise tools and trackers, to nutritionally helpful diet plans and logs. Most have the capability to post to your social networking accounts. I found these useful on a personal level because I was able to get positive reinforcement from my peers as well as have another way of tracking my progress.

Video Clips

In relation to the previous point, you may also look up video clips for additional inspiration. You may resort to videos with inspirational speeches or other similar content. If you do not have any idea on the types of video clips that you should watch, you may ask some people who are familiar with numerous types of clips. They can give you a good idea of what to check out.

There were days when I was completely bored with my workouts, the ones I had created and those that I had on DVD. Thanks to the internet, I could just look up the type of workout I wanted and do something new, interesting, and fun! There is every type of video workout imaginable out there on the World Wide Web. Thanks, Uncle Internet!

Vision Board

Don't put it off until tomorrow: start working on your vision board right now! Select the best pictures of your health and fitness idols and gurus, healthy foods, and motivational phrases! Include the pictures of clothes you want to wear and your ideal weight or fitness goals. Preparing a vision board is more powerful than you actually think. It will make you stop procrastinating and will also remind yourself of your wellness vision.

I kept one vision board on my refrigerator. It was visible from anywhere in my kitchen. That way, when preparing my meals, I was able to keep in mind the direction I was headed in. Motivation right in my face! Also I kept one in my home gym/workout area to boost <u>motivation and stamina</u> during my workouts.

Theme Song

Having different playlists for different forms of exercise was extremely useful in boosting motivation during my actual workouts. For running and fitness I would make a few playlists of fast-paced electronic music. You need music that sets you on fire. Music can be the best, natural source of "body and mind caffeine." Different people have different tastes. Prepare your own dynamic playlist.

This can even help you get rid of some calories that you gained from consuming your latest meal. Dance and jump energetically and burn all the calories while having fun and making your serotonin levels go up!

Walking, stretching, yoga, and "meditational" hiking playlists were full of more peaceful and mind-clearing music.

Farewell to Old Clothes

Visualizing how you will appear in the long run can help you stay motivated. In line with this, you should give away your larger clothes so you can pave the way for new smaller garments. Let go of the old and prepare yourself for the new! Aside from the actual size, try to change your style a bit. Experiment with new colors and designs. Express yourself. Reward yourself and celebrate your body and mind transformation!

CONCLUSION

Following your dreams, it is time for you to get committed to wellness and enjoy the process and finally the results of this commitment: more energy levels, sexy and fit body, more self-confidence, as well as more focus and zest for life.

Don't wait till New Year's, don't wait till tomorrow or next week ... do it now and let success come to YOU. Transform your body and transform your life the way you deserve it.

As they say- tomorrow never comes. You only have TODAY!

My personal opinion is that by not taking action, we create anxiety for ourselves. Think about it and how you can relate to it in different areas of your life.

Finally, if you enjoyed this book, please take the time to share your thoughts and post a review on Amazon.

It takes only a few seconds to post a review and your help would be greatly appreciated. If you have any questions, suggestions, or doubts, you can also contact me via e-mail at info@holisticwellnessproject.com

Thank you again for taking your time to read my book and good luck!

To your wellness success,

Marta

For more inspiration and empowerment, visit my blog:
www.HolisticWellnessProject.com
If you are interested in holistic nutrition, natural weight loss and alkaline diet lifestyle, check out my online course:
www.AlkalineDietLifestyle.com

Recommended Reading

Weight Loss: 2 in 1 Bundle-Special Edition of My Best Weight Loss Tips

That Do Not Require Torturing Yourself with Fads and Unrealistic Workout Programs!

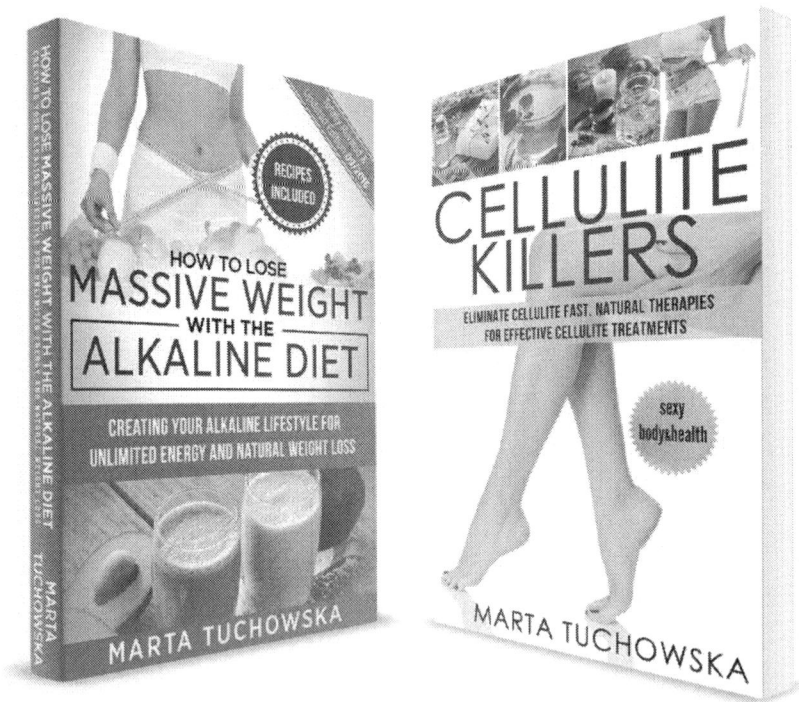

Kindle, paperback and even audio editions available in your local Amazon Store.

You will find more amazing health & wellness book deals at:

www.holisticwellnessproject.com/books

To your health,

Enjoy!

42128929R00054

Printed in Poland
by Amazon Fulfillment
Poland Sp. z o.o., Wrocław